ADIRONDACK COUNTING

A Counting Trip to the 46 Highest Peaks of the Adirondacks

Sheri Amsel

*A note to naturalists... We realize that although these animals are found in the Adirondacks, they would not likely congregate in groups as large as those depicted (with the exception of insects, footprints and pine cones!). This book is meant to improve counting skills, assist in learning about the mountains and animals of the Adirondack region and for just having fun finding hidden pictures. We hope you enjoy it...

For my sister, Laurel,
someone I can always "count" on...

North Country Books
311 Turner
Utica, NY 13501

ADIRONDACK COUNTING

A Counting Trip to the 46 Highest Peaks of the Adirondacks

Sheri Amsel

North Country Books
Utica, New York

1 mountain lion making tracks up Marcy.

2 aging aspens on the trail up Algonquin.

3 hungry hawks hunt hares over Haystack.

4 striped skunks search for supper on Skylight.

5 woodpeckers want woollybears on Whiteface.

6 white-tailed deer dine on dandelions on Dix.

7 great blue herons
glide gracefully over Gray.

8 idle insects in the irises on Iroquois.

9 burly bears bite berries on Basin.

10 gray foxes in a gang on Gothics.

11 creepy cobwebs catch critters on Colden.

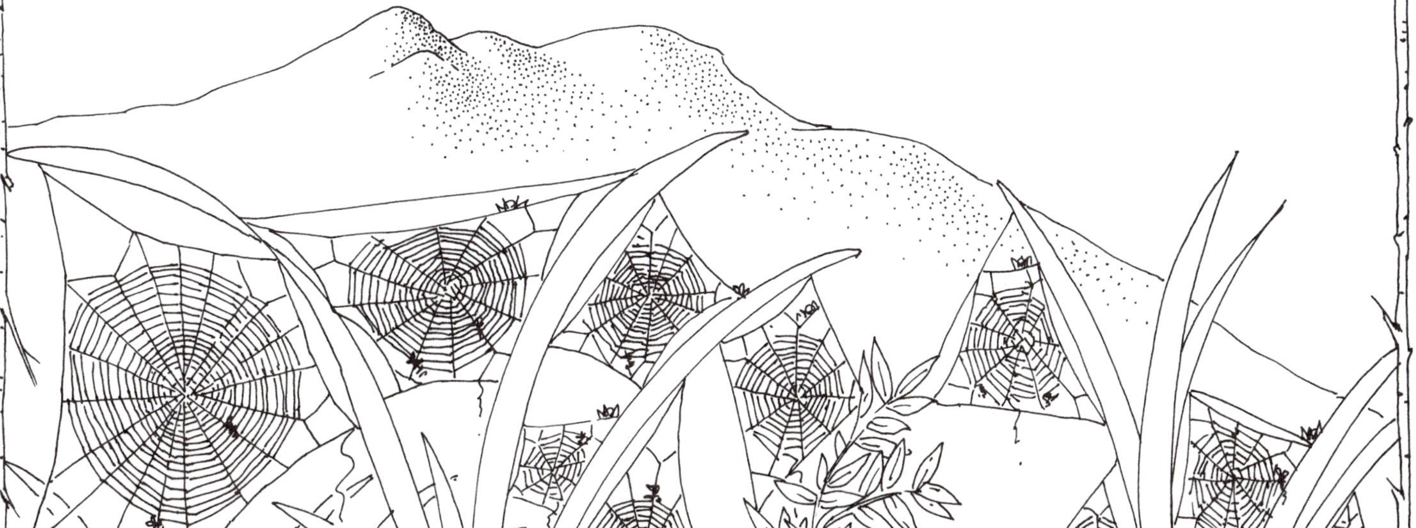

12 gray squirrels grab green grasshoppers on Giant.

13 northern orioles nibble nuts on Nipple Top.

14 saw-whet owls seek shelter on Santanoni.

15 rowdy raccoons raid raspberries on Redfield.

16 wood pewees wing westward on Wright.

17 snakes slither slowly on Saddleback.

18 poised peepers peeping peacefully on Panther.

19 tranquil turtles cover tree trunks on Tabletop.

20 river otters rummage rainbows on Rocky Ridge.

21 mice munch mushrooms on Macomb.

22 asters all alike on Armstrong.

23 hummingbirds hover on Hough.

24 sparrows sing sweetly on Seward.

25 moles mine meals on Marshall.

26 ants ascend
alders on Allen.

27 bees buzz bluebells
on Big Slide.

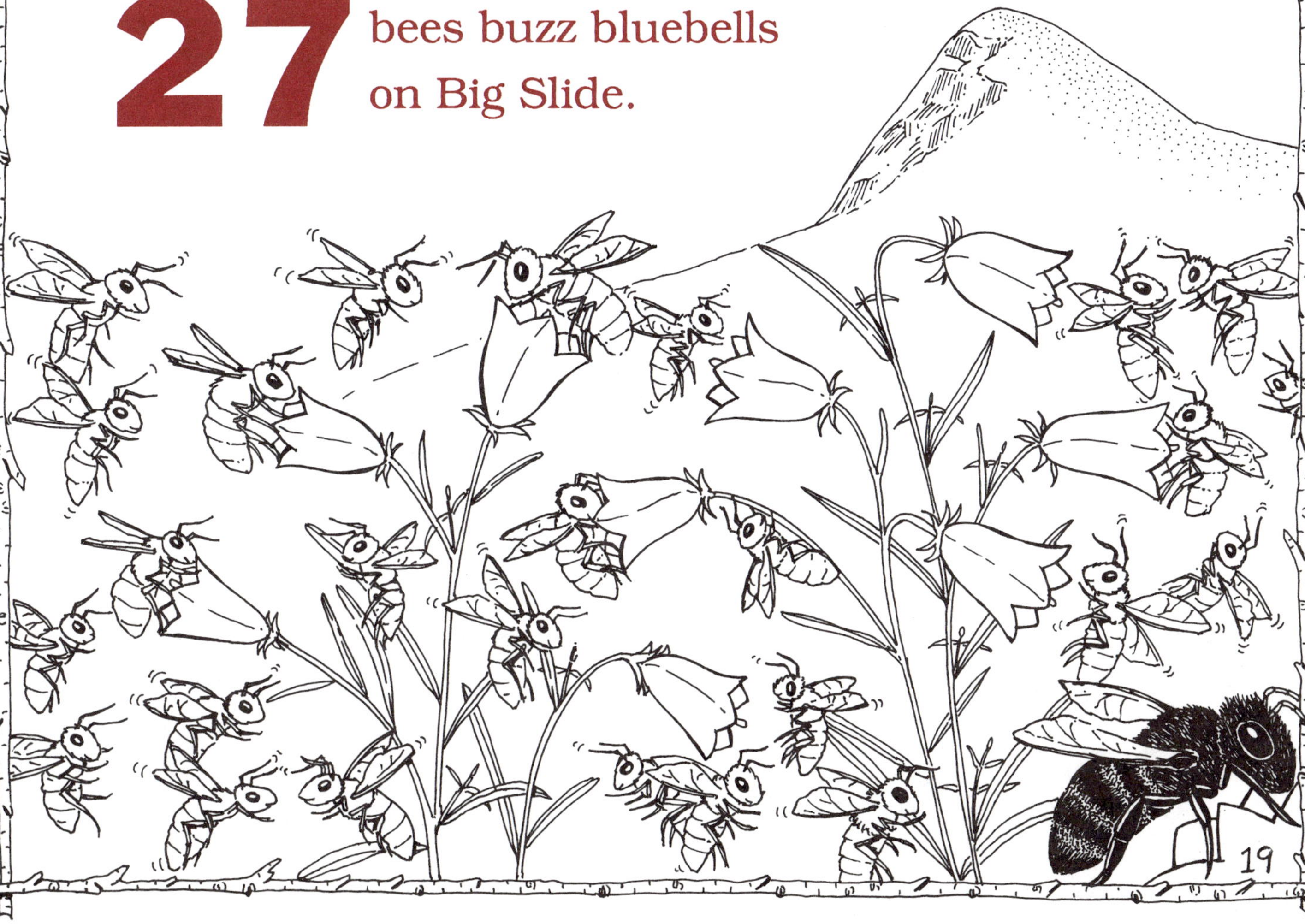

28 ermine explore edibles on Esther.

29 wood frogs in the willows on Upper Wolf Jaw.

30 lynx footprints left on Lower Wolf Jaw.

31 shrews scout for snacks on Street.

32 prickly porcupines pass time on Phelps.

33 daisies drift downwind on Donaldson.

34 snipes seen sailing over Seymour.

35 salamanders slink slowly on Sawteeth.

36 caterpillars crunch cherry trees on Cascade.

37 swallows swoop slowly on South Dix.

38 pine cones piled precariously on Porter.

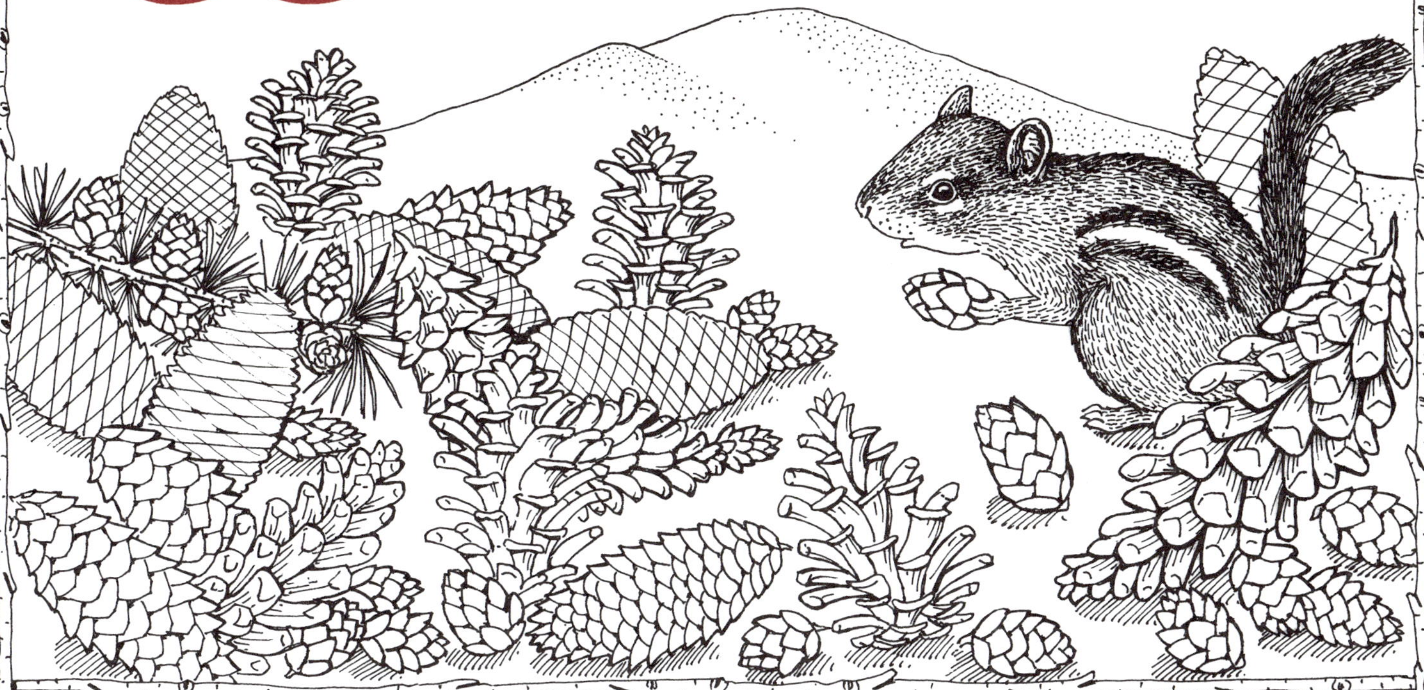

39 chickadees call their name on Colvin.

40 eastern chipmunks eat anything on Emmons.

41 dragonflies dart daringly on Dial.

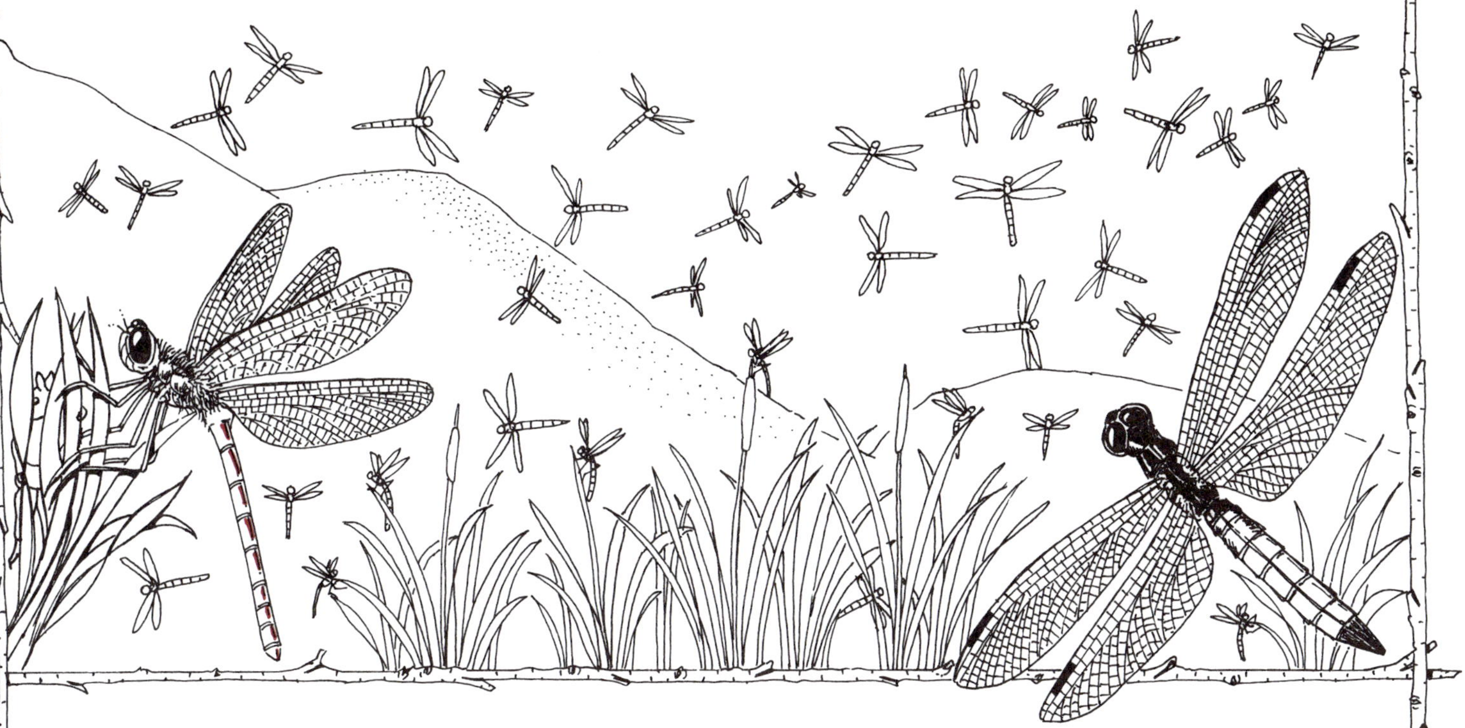

42 daddy long legs dance on East Dix.

43 big butterflies billow on Blake.

44 cottontails chew cowslips on Cliff.

45 newts nibble gnats on Nye.

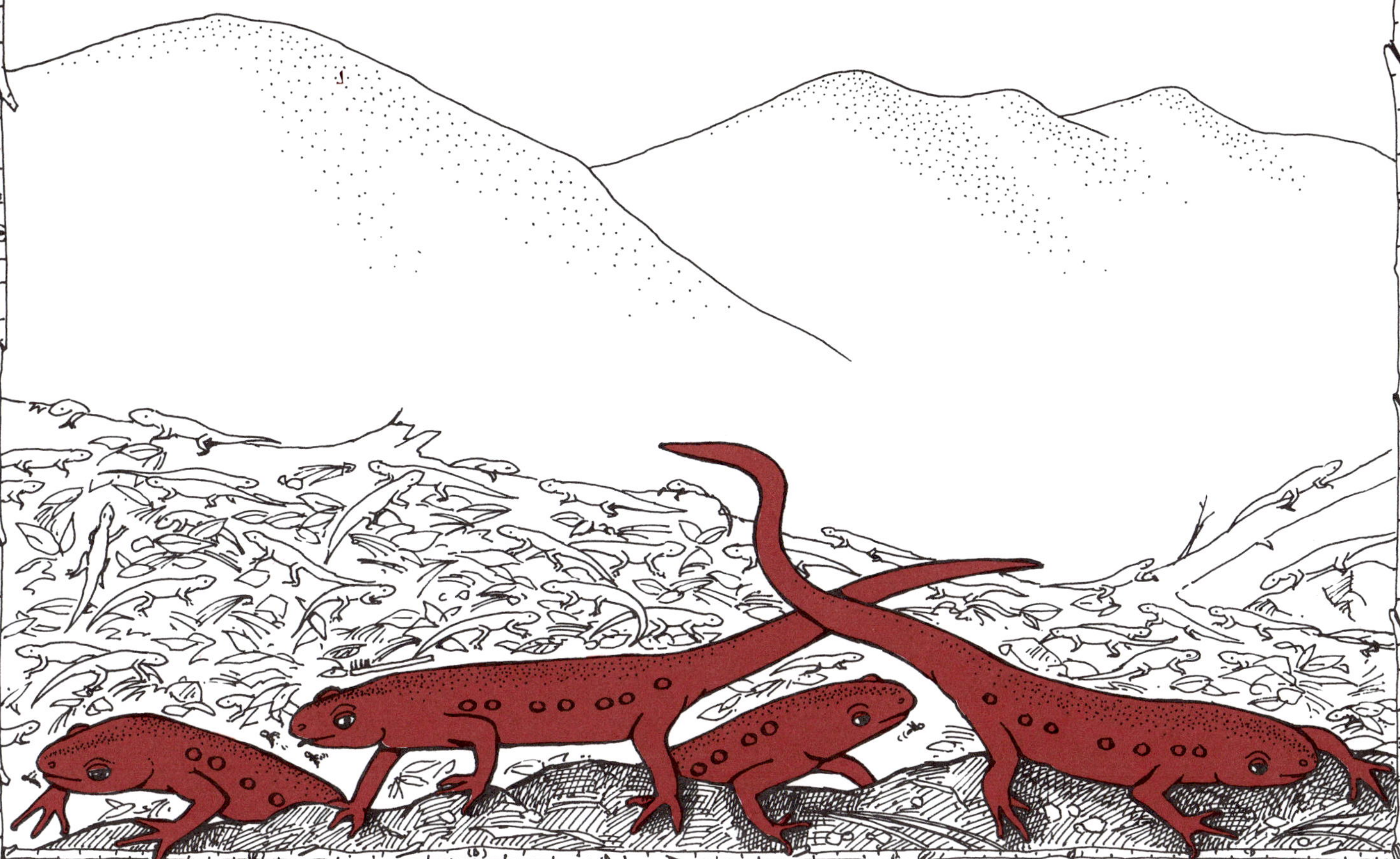

46 crickets chirp cheerfully on Coughsachraga.

Hey Kids...
Thanks for your help.
Hope you have a great
time exploring the
Adirondacks. It's a
great place, isn't it?
Cecil A. Mouse
MAP